Praise for Letti

"It was a pleasure to rea
many personal stories tra
picture. Each chapter brought unique insights. I really enjoyed the questions at the end of each chapter making it very personal.

"This book is easy to read and filled with some great quotes. 'No praise is a silent complaint' really struck home to me when read. 'Those who have both confidence and humility are authentic' showed the dynamics of a good life.

"The author points to the Biblical principle, 'Allow God to do what you cannot do for yourself.' Read this book and 'Let Go' for a better future."

Roy Waterhouse, President at Hopkins Printing

"This book can change your life. Each chapter is illustrated with a personal life experience which helps the reader to apply learned principles to his own life through challenging questions that make me think deeper. Whether you subscribe to a biblical worldview or not, this book can help you to get rid of roadblocks in your life that hold you back.

"I really enjoyed reading this well written, concise, and challenging book."

Uwe Romeike, Piano Teacher and Pianist

"Gripping personal examples show the merits of 'letting go.' The author provides type 'A' personalities a liberating path to achieving even more by 'letting go.' The book is a must read because it provides so much practical information in the context of a rich life and experiences."

John Miller, President and CEO of Superb Industries

"In this flowing and easy to ready book the author shares his personal experience where he comes close to losing his life. Addressing the importance of letting go by using his own or family's life experiences creates credibility and helped me to relate. If you feel like there is anything that may drag you down, you can benefit from one of the many letting go ideas."

Cem Ersahin, Program Manager

"It was a pleasure to read this book! Wow. So candid. So real! So inspiring."

Stacy Knox, MsED, Career Consultant and Consoler

"Great read for anyone challenged with worry and anxiety. Easy to read book with many practical examples of how 'letting go' can make a difference in your life. The story of his airplane pilot experience draws you in right away. So many of us try to control things in our life. The author does a great job of helping to see how letting go is actually the key to finding more peace. The book has a strong faith component and I recommend it to anyone with teenage or young adult children too, since so many young people today are challenged with anxiety and worry. This book provides good ways to re-order their thinking without 'preaching' at them."

Chris Hoban, Senior Service Delivery Manager

"This book is relevant to everyone and infused with so much wisdom. A must read for everyone… because we all need to let go of something."

Diahanna Vallentine, BCPA,
Oncology Financial Patient Advocate

Letting Go Saved My Life

How Letting Go Can Help You Grow

Reinhard Klett

Letting Go Saved My Life
By Reinhard Klett

ISBN: 978-0-578-69986-8

Cover and Interior Design by Transcendent Publishing

Printed in the United States of America.

Dedication

To the Lord, "Because You have been my help,
therefore in the shadow of Your wings I will rejoice"
(Psalm 63:7; NKJV)

Table of Contents

Introduction

Have you ever felt stuck, unable to make progress in your personal and spiritual growth, because you were holding onto things that were no longer working, or perhaps never worked at all? If so, you are invited to read more.

A very close brush with death while a student pilot in my early thirties greatly changed my outlook on life. It began a process of reevaluating how I was living and weeding out those things that had been holding me back. Whenever I shared this story over the years, people would invariably tell me that it inspired them to also let go of things and move forward in their lives.

It was a typical Southern California day in June of 1990. A few minutes earlier, I had taken off from Van Nuys Airport on my third solo flight in a two-seater Cessna 150. Below me, the hills around Simi Valley shimmered a golden brown in the desert sun, a beautiful sight to behold.

It was over Simi Valley that I would practice one of the most dangerous flight maneuvers: an approach to landing stall recovery. As the name suggests, this maneuver is practiced at a high altitude to make sure there is room for recovery if anything goes wrong.

"Burbank Approach," I said into the radio, "this is Cessna One Five Zero Golf Sierra. I am a student pilot and will practice approach to landing stall recovery over Simi Valley at twenty-five hundred feet. Please advise of any approaching aircraft."

I knew exactly what to do, having practiced this maneuver many times with Paul, my flight instructor. But this time was different. I was all by myself, with no flight instructor to take the controls if something went wrong. I could not make any mistakes. With sweaty palms, I prepared the maneuver. After rocking the plane to make sure there are no other aircraft under me or near me, I pulled the control wheel to reduce the air speed. To maintain altitude, I pushed in the throttle a little; then, to simulate a landing approach, I lowered the flaps – first fifteen degrees, then thirty and, finally, forty-five degrees. I maintained a straight and level flight, pulling the wheel closer and closer towards me. The air speed was getting down towards the stall speed of forty-two knots in landing configuration and the stall warning horn went off. Now the plane felt very unstable. In order to practice a quick recovery, I pulled the wheel even closer to further reduce the air speed, stalling the plane. Everything was going according to plan.

At this point I was expecting the nose to drop, but – what is this? – the left wing dropped before the right wing did. My heart was in my stomach as I realized I had inadvertently gotten myself into a downward spiral, also known as "the graveyard spiral." Before me, the ground was spinning like a disk. The hand on the altimeter kept turning, showing the rapid descent. The airspeed indicator had rapidly climbed from forty-two knots to one hundred-twenty knots. The realization that these will be the last few seconds of my life flashed through my mind.

Then my survival instinct kicked in. I immediately pulled the throttle to avoid additional downward acceleration by the engine, then pulled in the flaps to protect them from bending or breaking at this high speed. But nothing I did had any effect. A thought to call the tower to ask for help was quickly dismissed; there was simply not enough time.

To live through this would take a miracle...

And with that thought, I took my hands off the wheel and my feet off the pedals, and cried out, "God take this plane!!"

In an instant, the plane got out of the downward spiral and into a straight and level flight. A look at the altimeter told me that within seconds I had gone from twenty-five hundred feet down to fifteen hundred feet above the ground. I just dropped one thousand feet! I knew that had I held onto the controls any longer I would have run myself right into the ground. I had to let go of the controls completely and let God take over. He was the only one who could get me out of this life-threatening situation, and He did.

Today, I look back on this terrifying experience as the biggest blessing of my life. And while this is (hopefully) a more drastic wakeup call than most people receive, its lesson, I believe, is applicable to any situation in which we need to let go of something. When we try to control situations, we often make them worse. When we let God take over, miracles happen. We should see God, not as a copilot to be called upon only in times of distress, but our captain, all the time.

Remember what the Psalmist has written:

"Call upon Me in the day of trouble; I will deliver you, and you shall glorify Me" (Psalm 50:15; NKJV).

"As for me, I will call upon God, And the LORD shall save me" (Psalm 55:16; NKJV).

In the following chapters, you will be challenged to reflect upon and let go of whatever is holding you back. By no means is this an exhaustive list of the types of "baggage" people carry, but it is my hope that it will help you begin the process of excavating your mind and heart. At times you may be surprised by what you have been carrying around like a sack of bricks over your shoulder. You may also feel like you've been carrying that sack around for so long you will never be able to set it down. Again, keep reading, for I will show you the tools to remove the clutter from your mind and see the truth of who you are meant to be.

At the end of each chapter you will be asked questions to contemplate and journal about. These are the same types of questions I ask my coaching clients, and some of them will be uncomfortable and cut right to the heart. Just know that they are not meant to hurt or judge, but to challenge you to reflect deeply on your journey and identify areas for potential growth. They are designed to help you come to "Aha" moments and breakthroughs that will change your life.

CHAPTER 1

Letting Go of Control

It is human nature to crave stability in our lives, whether it concerns our finances and relationships, our physical safety and even our daily habits. For example, I like our house to be clean, orderly and everything in good repair. For many of us, stability has become synonymous with control; we like to think that if we are running the show, nothing can go wrong. However, as illustrated in the story of my near crash, this couldn't be further from the truth.

I tend to be one of those people; when things are out of control, I am outside of my comfort zone. I had to learn through experience that in some situations trying to keep things under our control can only make it worse.

I recall the time my wife and I were on our way to the airport in Knoxville, Tennessee to catch a flight to Atlanta; from there we would connect to a flight to Florida, where we were attending the Feast of Tabernacles. As we pulled out of our subdivision in Morristown, my wife looked at the flight itinerary and realized that the time she thought we would leave Knoxville was actually the time we were supposed to arrive in Atlanta. There was no way we would make it to the first leg of our flight. I knew then that this was a big test of my attitude. I had no control over the departure times, but I could control my thoughts and emotions and not let the frustration get the better of me. I knew that if I did not pass this test, we would certainly not make it down to Florida in time for the opening night of the Feast. I would also be giving added stress to my wife, who had made an honest mistake and could not do anything to fix it. I decided I would not get upset with her, and she did what she normally does in situations like that: she prayed. We got to the airport and caught the next flight to Atlanta and, guess what? When we touched down in Georgia, the plane to Florida was still standing there! The test was not over, though, because we were then bumped off the second leg of our flight, and it was overbooked! I asked the attendant in the boarding area if she could put us on the waiting list, gently trying to get her sympathy as we had our son, who was not quite two years old, with us. She said she would do what she could to help us out. We were the last three people to board that plane.

The point to this story: being a hard-nosed control freak who has to get his way would not have helped the situation. It only would have made it stressful, exhausting and embarrassing for everybody. Being demanding with the representative at the gate probably would have made her less cooperative, and chances are we would have never made it to Florida that evening. This had clearly been a test of how I would respond to an inconvenient and frustrating situation, and I had passed!

In situations like that it helps us to remember the admonition of the Apostle James: "My brethren, count it all joy when you fall into various trials, knowing that the testing of your faith produces patience" (James 1:2, NKJV). Instead of being frustrated, we can look at each situation as a learning and testing opportunity.

And even if we do miss a flight, who knows, there may be a reason and a purpose. Learning to trust that things will work out, even when they do not work out the way we expected, we can rest in the assurance "...that all things work together for good to those who love God, to those who are the called according to [His] purpose," (Romans 8:28, NKJV).

There are many things beyond our control – the wind and the weather, other people and a whole host of circumstances – but we can learn to control ourselves, and how we set the sail in response to each challenging situation.

This is common sense, but unfortunately not so common a practice. I know, because giving up control of circumstances is not something that comes naturally for me, thus I continuously need to remind myself to shift my focus to controlling my own reaction to them.

I find it helps to think about those situations *before* we get into them. The more we can think about them rationally, rather than reacting to them emotionally, the more we are trusted and respected by other people. The more we are respected, the more influence we have, which usually yields much better results than our attempts to control. The more we practice controlling ourselves, the more our influence will grow. Then a lot more things will go the way we hope them to go without being demanding, manipulative and unpleasant in the process.

Questions to ask yourself:

- What situations have I been in that I tried to control and only made things worse?

- Have I ever been in situations when I stepped back and did not try to control things and it all worked out just fine?

- Are there situations right now in my life when it would be best to just let go of control?

- What would I tell myself in the future when I find myself in a stressful or frustrating situation?

- What would the best response be if I acted rationally and in faith?

CHAPTER 2

Letting Go of Fears and Worries

Fears and worries are something we all deal with in our lives. However, if we can learn to let go of them, they do not have to become our slave masters.

Of course, there are situations when we are exposed to real physical dangers, like when thirty-five elephants crossed the gravel road in front of me as I drove through the Etosha National Park in Namibia, South West Africa. Or when a rhino came uncomfortably close to my Volkswagen Beetle. Or when I was in that graveyard spiral, I told you about earlier. In those situations, our fear can help protect us; in fact, this is what are our natural "fight or flight" response system was designed to do.

However, most fears and worries we entertain on a daily basis are not those that protect us from real physical harm. Rather, they are related to things we imagine in our minds. For example, one of the greatest fears that many people have is the fear of public speaking.

Imagine for a moment that you are standing before a crowd of people, all waiting to hear what you have to say. If this conjures a feeling of fear, it is likely because you are afraid of leaving a bad impression, or at least not as good an impression as you hope for. You are making yourself a slave to the opinions of others. This fear greatly increases the chances that you will be very nervous when you do speak. You will not be as focused on the speech as you could be, or you talk so fast that the audience has a hard time following you. The fear becomes a self-fulfilling prophecy. The fear diminishes your performance, which affects the impression you want to leave.

So how do you let go of that fear? Let's look at the nature of the fear itself.

The fear is created in our own minds because we focus on ourselves. In case of public speaking, the focus is on leaving a good impression, which may be critical if the speech is given in a professional setting, and thus may affect our career. That is understandable. So, how do we deal with that? What must shift in our minds? When I was in college, I took a class in public speaking. The professor told us that the way to overcome the fear of public speaking is by shifting our focus away from leaving a good impression to providing as much value as possible to the audience. When we cultivate an attitude of service, the natural consequence will be a much better impression. When the audience feels that you care for them and are not self-absorbed, you will win them over. They won't care whether your execution was flawless because their focus will be on the value you provided them.

An audience can smell inauthenticity or arrogance from a mile away. When we are being real, rather than pretending to be perfect or like we know it all, we will have a much more positive influence and impact. When we strive for progress and growth in our public speaking ability, rather than leaving that perfect impression, our fear evaporates.

The same rule applies with regard to most fears we have around social interactions. The best way to overcome such fears is to focus on developing genuine goodwill and love towards other people. If we do this and act with integrity, striving to become our best self, we will grow in confidence. When we are more confident, we become less self-conscious, less easily offended and as a result much more enjoyable to be around.

Focusing on genuine love for others will cast out many a fear and worry. Letting go of thoughts about what could go wrong and instead embracing loving thoughts and a positive outlook will not only lead to a lot more freedom, it will generate the kind of productive, creative energy that enables us to deal with any challenges.

Letting go of fear and worry is not instantaneous, but a process that takes place in our minds. Just as I had to decide how to deal with the frustration of missing our flight to Atlanta, we can all choose how we deal with the thoughts of fear and worry that enter our minds on a regular basis. It all comes down to how much weight, importance and duration we give those thoughts.

There are three points that have helped me to deal with fears, worries and anxieties, particularly in 2009, when I faced a challenging transition in my life. Before that I had never really had to worry about economic security. Then the Great Recession hit, resulting in a major downturn in the automotive industry. In the spring of that year, I was laid off and given a severance package that covered only six months of my salary. With my wife at home, homeschooling our two boys, my family depended on my income to survive. It was like a real punch in the gut, and a real challenge to maintain a positive and optimistic outlook and not be overcome and paralyzed by fear.

1. Consider the consequences of fear and worry.

During this time, I began to think about and evaluate the impact my fears and worries were having on my mind and my life. This was quite a wakeup call, and I realized how important it was to let go of those fears and worries. I had to make a conscious effort to think rationally about the situation.

- Worry keeps our focus on the problem and prevents us from looking at possible solutions.
- Worry negatively impacts our mood. "Anxiety in the heart of man causes depression, but a good word makes it glad" (Proverbs 12:25; NKJV). I knew that if I got into a depression over this situation, it would make matters a lot worse.
- "There is no fear in love; but perfect love casts out fear, because fear involves torment. But he who fears has not been made perfect in love" (1 John 4:18; NKJV). Think about this in light of our earlier example, the fear of public speaking. If we have love for our audience, we will be focused on delivering value and providing

service. Perfect love does not concern itself with an impression or an image we leave behind.

- Worry is self-sabotage. It is paralyzing. Fear is the greatest slave master; it keeps us caged. Almost all bad decisions are made based on fear. When fear reigns, rational thinking usually goes out the window.

2. Fear is a form of disobedience to God.

There are plenty of logical reasons for not giving into fear. However, if they are not enough to produce a shift in our mind, maybe our reverence and respect towards God will motivate us to let go of fear and worry. I know it did for me.

We are commanded by Jesus Christ, "Do not worry" (Matthew 6:25, NKJV).

We are also encouraged to have a positive and optimistic outlook by the Apostle Paul. While in prison, he wrote: "Be anxious for nothing, but in everything by prayer and supplication, with thanksgiving, let your requests be made known to God; and the peace of God, which surpasses all understanding, will guard your hearts and minds through Christ Jesus. Finally, brethren, whatever things are true, whatever things [are] noble, whatever things [are] just, whatever things [are] pure, whatever things [are] lovely, whatever things [are] of good report, if [there is] any virtue and if [there is] anything praiseworthy – meditate on these things" (Philippians, 4:6-8, NKJV).

After losing my job I had to read these passages over and over each day in order to really internalize them.

Many of us feel like a certain level of anxiety keeps us on our toes; however, it does not help us to be calm, patient, and hopeful. When I am tempted to be anxious, I remind myself of what the Apostle Paul told Timothy: "For God has not given us a spirit of fear, but of power and of love and of a sound mind" (2 Timothy 1:7; NKJV). This takes me out of panic and into alignment with the way God would want me to think.

3. Facing our fears.

If we shift our thinking from what we fear to what we can achieve, we will be able to act with more courage, despite those fears. For example, after getting into that graveyard spiral, I was scared to get back on that plane again. I had a choice to make, overcome the fear or give up on my dream of getting a private pilot license. I chose the former. That same day, after my adrenaline level came back down, I did three solo takeoffs and landings.

I learned this lesson from my father when I was very young. One Sunday afternoon, my Aunt Ursula came to our house for a visit. On her way back to her house, she got into a car accident which thankfully resulted in no serious injuries but totaled her car. Aunt Ursula was at fault, and my father was concerned that she would be afraid to get behind the wheel again. To help her through this situation, he took her to a car dealership the very next day so she could get her new car. That's what I remembered when I sat in the pilot's lounge at Van Nuys Airport the afternoon I first got back onto the plane.

Overcoming our fears is a constant struggle in our minds. We have a choice: either we give in to our fears and become slaves to them, or we embrace the struggle and fight for the liberty that comes from overcoming fear.

Questions to ask yourself:

- What are some of the fears and worries in my life that I have not yet let go of?

  ____
  ____
  ____
  ____
  ____
  ____
  ____

- What is keeping me from letting them go?

  ____
  ____
  ____
  ____
  ____
  ____
  ____

- What are the reasons I tell myself for holding on to them?

  ____
  ____
  ____
  ____
  ____
  ____
  ____
  ____

- What fears have I been able to face and overcome in my life?

____
____
____
____
____
____

- What helped me to face those fears?

____
____
____
____
____
____

- What helped me to overcome those fears?

____
____
____
____
____
____

- How can I apply the same strategies to the fears and worries I am still dealing with today?

____
____
____
____
____
____
____

CHAPTER 3

Letting go of (Ego) Pride

When I was growing up in Germany, modesty and humility were taught as virtues and pride was frowned upon, particularly the national pride that was squelched in the Post-World War II era. It therefore struck me as strange when I came to America, first as an exchange student and later as a permanent resident, to see pride often treated as a virtue. I was especially surprised to hear expressions of pride in Christian circles, because every time you see the word pride in the Bible, it is viewed in a negative light.

A bit of research revealed that the only application of the word pride in the Bible is about ego-pride, arrogance, and haughtiness, in other words, all its negative synonyms.

However, when I looked at various dictionaries, I realized that the English word pride has many positive synonyms, such as honor, respect, confidence and dignity.

So why let go of pride? What is the problem?

Well, for one, pride often robs us of our objectivity. Here is an example:

A few years ago, when I worked as a program manager for a global automotive supplier, I had some visitors from our sister company in China. Our day of meetings began with a presentation in which they talked about their country's history. They brought up World War II, including the war crimes committed by the Japanese during the Rape of Nanjing, which resulted in the deaths of approximately two hundred thousand Chinese. They also expressed gratitude to the United States for liberating China from the Japanese invasion.

That evening, dinner with our colleagues yielded some interesting discussions. When the topic turned to national pride, I explained the problem I saw with it, based on what I was taught growing up in Germany after the War. Indeed, it was extreme nationalism that led to much of the evil committed by the Nazi regime. I told them that we constantly need to be on guard against it, lest history repeat itself. We then talked about their presentation that morning, when they mentioned what the Japanese had done to them. But what, I asked them, of the millions of people who were killed by their own people during Mao's Cultural Revolution that followed World War II? Needless to say, that question gave them pause.

The problem with national pride is that it robs us of our objectivity. We remember very well the atrocities that others have committed against our people, but we are quick to overlook how badly our own people have treated us, or others for that matter.

The same can be said of personal pride. Pride always seems to be concerned with how we are being viewed by others. We want to impress them, and oftentimes compromise our principles of honesty and truth in the process.

How about "good" pride? As mentioned above, there are a plethora of synonyms for pride, both positive and negative, but to me, they do not provide for real clarity of mind. And, as we use language to express our thoughts, when the words are not clear our thinking can be a bit foggy as well.

For example, when a parent says, "I am proud of my child," the assumption is that they are using the word proud to describe their feelings of gratitude, happiness, joy and love for their children.

On the other hand, hidden in this expression could be a spirit of competition and self-righteousness, such as, "My kid performs so much better than the other kid" or, "My kid is not as bad as so many other kids."

In this case parents can check their own attitude by asking themselves whether it would be just as easy to say to another kid who had just beaten their own in a competition, "I am proud of you"? If not, we know this is an ego-pride situation.

The way in which I gain clarity in my own mind, and clearly express myself to others, is to avoid using the word pride when I mean something positive. Our Heavenly Father gives us a good example when He said about Jesus Christ, "This is my beloved Son, in whom I am well pleased" (Matthew 3:18; NKJV), as did the apostle John when he said, "I have no greater joy than to hear that my children walk in truth" (3 John 1:4; NKJV)

Similarly, when I express feelings of gratitude, joy or happiness, I prefer to use those words instead of the word pride. That way there is no ambiguity, for myself or whoever I am speaking to. This also helps children understand these concepts correctly. For example, the child will not make the assumption that, "My parents are proud of me, so it is okay to be proud."

Understanding Humility

The word humility also seems to be much more clearly expressed in the Bible than in the common vernacular. It is used in several ways, all of them the exact opposite of pride, for example:

- Unconditional obedience and submission to God (as Noah, Abraham, Job, Daniel and his friends, and others demonstrated when pressured to disobey Him).
- Being teachable by God, as Solomon was in the beginning. Even when we are good at something there is always room to grow and learn.
- Admitting our own sins and shortcomings (as King David did, when he was confronted by the prophet Nathan).
- Not blaming others for our disobedience (as King Saul did when he blamed the people, when He did not fully obey God's instructions).
- Admitting and confessing our complete dependence on God (when we fast, for example).

Even though the Bible appears to be pretty clear about the meaning of humility, the English dictionary provides many synonyms, which I believe to be characteristics of a false humility, such as self-hate, self-disgust, self-loathing, bashfulness, shyness, timidity, passiveness, unassertiveness, docility, non-resistance, resignation, inferiority complex, being reserved, being poor, et cetera.

So, if we are striving to be humble, where do our thoughts go to? Are we focusing on Biblical examples of true humility, or are we mistakenly thinking we are humble because we have bought into the definitions above, which indicate, for the most part, a lack of self-worth?

Confidence:

As opposed to (ego-) pride, confidence is a good character trait.

A lack of confidence (low self-esteem) can create a lot of problems. You have seen this in people. Having little confidence creates a void they often fill with pride, which shows when they get easily offended, while at the same time they can be very critical and condescending of others.

I am well acquainted with low self-esteem, having struggled with confidence as a kid. I was held back a year in elementary school because I had meningitis in the third grade. Also, I was not athletic, usually the last kid to be chosen when teams were selected for ball games and struggled to get a passing mark in English as a foreign language class in the fifth grade. It wasn't until my teenage years, when I joined the Boy Scouts, that I started to develop more confidence.

When we look at the great men in the Bible and many others in history, we see that they had one thing in common: They possessed both great confidence (not pride) and authentic humility.

- Moses had great humility with respect to God yet was a bold leader of the children of Israel.
- David expressed great humility before God while showing great confidence and boldness when faced with Goliath.
- The Apostle Paul showed great humility before God when he accepted the trials he went through, yet he showed great confidence and boldness when he faced the Romans and addressed issues in the churches he worked with.

When we understand the difference between pride and confidence, we do not have to be afraid of being confident. We can have strong confidence and humility at the same time. Actually, confidence can only grow with humility. If you are humble, you are teachable and will continue to learn and grow, which in turn increases your confidence. On the other hand, if you are proud and lack the humility to grow and learn, your confidence decreases, and you become defensive when challenged.

So, what can we do if we struggle with confidence?

- Get our minds off ourselves. The universe does not revolve around us.
- Forget about what other people may think of us. Usually they do not think about us nearly as much as we think anyway.

- Meditate on God – what He has done for you, for example, the sacrificing of His son.

  Thus says the LORD: "Let not the wise [man] glory in his wisdom, Let not the mighty [man] glory in his might, Nor let the rich [man] glory in his riches; But let him who glories glory in this, That he understands and knows Me, That I [am] the LORD, exercising lovingkindness, judgment, and righteousness in the earth. For in these I delight," says the LORD (Jeremiah 9:23; NKJV).

  Realize that our identity is that of a child of God, a child who is not perfect but strives to please God, strives to bring Him joy by making the greatest possible contributions to glorify Him.

  "I can do all things through Christ who strengthens me" (Philippians 4:13; NKJV).

- Help others develop confidence, and in the process, you will develop more confidence yourself.

  Praise others, especially children. This is not false praise (flattery) which results in low standards and mediocrity. True recognition of one's gifts, in combination with setting high expectations and boundaries, helps people fulfil their potential. If we do not praise our children, they will fall for the first predator who does.

  I grew up in a culture in which it was said that "No complaint is enough praise." This is based on the completely unfounded fear that praise leads to pride and arrogance, when I find that just the opposite is true.

  My wife and I talked about this and turned this phrase inside out. We find that,

"No praise is a silent complaint."

- In social settings, focus less on yourself and focus more on the people you talk to. Ask what they have to say. Do not worry about "performing," or thinking about all the things you could say to make you look smart. Just find out what you could learn from somebody else and they will love you! Do not take it personally when they do not agree with you. Just make sure you are aligned with God, without trying to assume responsibility for making sure others are.

Now back to dealing with our pride. As mentioned above, replacing pride with other words helps me to be clear in my mind, and confidence is one of those words. When I think of confidence, I think of knowing what is right, knowing my Creator and striving to please Him by living in harmony with His principles and values. This way I am free of what other people think; I am free to be my best self – happy, satisfied and content.

While pride and humility cannot coexist in the biblical sense of the words; confidence and humility can. So, when we strive to guard our minds against thoughts and attitudes which do not serve us, it helps to ask ourselves:

Why do I feel good about something? Why am I uplifted?

I feel good when I have thought and acted in harmony with my highest ideals and principles. This is confidence, and it still leaves me open to do better the next time, still open to personal growth.

If, on the other hand, I feel good because I bested somebody in a competition, impressed them, or made them jealous, I am being prideful. This creates an arrogant sense of superiority, and a false sense of confidence. Why get better, when I am already the best? Growth and authenticity are stunted, and an "us-vs-them" mindset develops. Groupthink reigns. It's like a magnifying glass for all the "great" things we have accomplished, and all the "bad" things other people have done, while diminishing our own flaws and the good qualities of others. Pride makes us judge ourselves by our best intentions and others by their worst actions.

As mentioned earlier, our thoughts are expressed by the words we use. To have clarity in our minds, it helps us to use words that are clear and unambiguous.

So, the next time you feel proud, consider letting it go and embracing confidence and humility instead. This will help you become more objective, authentic, less easily offended and free to be your best self with anybody you meet.

Questions to ask yourself:

- Where has my ego stood in the way of my personal growth?

  ____
  ____
  ____
  ____
  ____
  ____
  ____

- What blind spots do I have about myself because of my pride?

- How has my pride stood in the way of developing deeper and trusting relationships?

- Do I think that I am humble because I am shy, poor, lack confidence, lack skill, lack resources?

- Or am I actually humble because I reflect on myself and see my shortcomings, no matter how successful I may be?

- Am I teachable and willing to learn, even from those I may not look up to?

- Do I lack confidence because I compare myself with others? If so, pride may be the issue.

- What steps could I take to develop confidence with humility?
    - Self-Confidence: Do I realize how much my Creator loves me and values me?
    - Social Confidence: Am I developing social skills, taking my mind off myself and focusing on others? Do I courageously face my fears and approach people?
    - Confidence in our competence: Do I continue to expand my skills and abilities to contribute more, or am I standing still when it comes to my skill development?

CHAPTER 4

Letting Go of Habits Which Do Not Serve Us

Have you ever felt bad about particular habits you cannot seem to kick? If so, you are not alone.

Humans tend to be creatures of habit. Much of what we do every day and much of how we respond to different situations in life is based on habits we have established over time. Many of our habits developed while we were growing up, by imitating people around us; they seemed to make sense and eventually became our comfort zone. These habits also have a huge impact on the way our lives turn out. They affect our health, our well-being, our relationships, and how well we do in our work. Some habits are good, leading to happiness, success, maturity and prosperity, while others have the opposite effect. You know where I am going with this.

If we want our lives to move into a more positive direction; if we want to be in better health, have deeper relationships, and to be a force for good in the world, we need to let go of those habits that do not serve us or anyone else.

To let go of bad habits, we need to be more intentional about how we live our lives.

Like everyone, I emulated my parents while growing up and picked up some habits from them as well. My father had wine or beer with dinner, and as an adult I started doing the same; sometimes I didn't stop at one but had two or three. In my mind this habit was associated with relaxing after a hard day at work, taking the edge off a bit, which I felt I deserved. Though it did bring me short-term comfort, however, I was not very useful after dinner. I would spend the evenings watching TV or engaging in other unproductive activities. This would also often lead to late night snacks, which of course was not helpful in maintaining a healthy body weight.

The week after my parent's golden wedding anniversary my father was diagnosed with pancreatic cancer; he died eight months later at the age of seventy-seven. I did not realize until later that my father's nightly habit of having a beer or wine with dinner had, after his retirement, developed into a habit of drinking a whole bottle of wine each night. He never seemed drunk or got out of line and, since he did not have to perform a job anymore, his alcohol consumption never appeared to create much of a problem. After doing a little bit of research, however, I learned that drinking a bottle of wine every night was very likely one of the big contributors to the development of his pancreatic cancer.

This made me look at my own drinking, and I came to the conclusion that the habit was worse than I had realized. Although

I had often gone without alcohol for several days, I decided it was not serving me well and I had to let it go, if only to prove to myself and my wife that I was not an alcoholic. To relieve tension, I began looking for alternative solutions, such as just laying down to relax for ten to twenty minutes and drinking some soothing tea after work. I soon found that I had more productive hours in the day as well as better sleep at night.

My younger son Daniel, who has never picked up the habit of drinking alcohol, has been of great encouragement and inspiration to me in this regard. Daniel, who is very fit and healthy, has this simple motto: "Alcohol has no proteins, only empty calories, so why drink it?"

Letting go of bad habits takes effort. It requires a shift in thinking, both about what we are giving up by breaking the habit and what we will gain. Keeping these, as well as our commitment to break the habit, forefront in our minds will help keep us on track when we find ourselves in tempting situations.

Three things that have helped me break tough habits are:

1. Thinking of negative consequences.

Thinking through the negative effects our habits have on our health, relationships, productivity, and our ability to serve and fulfil our dreams is an important first step. Think about the consequences today, next week, next year, and five or ten years down the road. Becoming fully aware of the negative consequences of our habits oftentimes requires a deeper understanding; for example, if we want to give up sugar, we need to educate ourselves about all the negative consequences on our health and then ask ourselves whether that momentary pleasure is worth the pain. A good friend of mine has lost a leg to diabetes. Is changing our eating habits worth keeping our legs? You know the answer.

2. Focus on the gain, rather than the pain

Think about the positive consequences of getting rid of a bad habit. Think about all the things you can do and enjoy, and how it will make you feel in the long term. Know your "why" for making this positive change in your life and think about it often. Write it down and put it on your fridge, on your desk, your calendar, wherever you are sure to see it often. You can also set up an alarm on your cell phone with words that remind you one, two or three times a day. (If you don't know how to do that, Google it or ask any tech-savvy teenager.)

3. Replacing the bad habits with good habits.

If you're trying to cut down on your coffee, replace it with some tea (green tea would be ideal). Instead of having a beer, drink a soothing tea to relax. Remember that coffee and beer are acquired tastes, just as all things that are bitter. Try instead to acquire a taste for things that are good for you.

We maintain many of our habits because there is a certain void in our lives. Subconsciously, we try to fill that void because we don't realize that there is only one who can truly do this: Our Creator, who gives us purpose.

Overcoming habits is a battle between the spirit and the flesh, which even the great spiritual leaders such as the Apostle Paul had to fight. (Romans 7:13-25 NKJV)

When the struggle is strong, it will require much praying and fasting. Fasting takes it down to the physiological level, as much of our habits have become ingrained in our brains. Do some research on healthy fasting, and if prudent, ask your doctor about it.

Bad habits often send our lives into a downward spiral just as surely as my plane did that day. And like that fateful flight, the spiral may seem impossible to get out of. But with the help of God and through complete surrender to Him, we can let go and let Him take over. Nothing feels better and is more liberating than to be carried in the loving arms of our Creator.

Questions to ask yourself:

- What habits do I have that I know, or suspect have a negative impact on my health? Which three of these habits could I drop?

  ____
  ____
  ____
  ____
  ____
  ____

- What habits could I adopt that would improve my health? What three habits could I implement right away that would have a positive impact?

  ____
  ____
  ____
  ____
  ____
  ____

- What value do I put on my health? How high is my ambition to get as healthy as I can be, and why?

____
____
____
____
____
____
____
____

- How does my health impact the service I can provide for others?

____
____
____
____
____
____
____
____

- If my health were poor, how much of a burden would that put on my family, my friends, my neighbors, and my finances?

____
____
____
____
____
____
____

- Do I have habits that negatively affect my relationships? Are good relationships worth letting go of those habits?

- What habits do I have that reduce my level of productivity? What distracts me or slows me down? Work is a big part of our lives and being productive means that we can serve at a higher level. What habits do I need to let go of in order to increase my contribution?

- What other habit(s) in my life do I know I should get rid of?

- If I am not getting rid of those habits, what is holding me back? What beliefs, fears and excuses am I holding onto that keep me from letting go?

- Am I willing to step out of my comfort zone for a while so that I can get out of that downward spiral my bad habit is taking me on?

CHAPTER 5

Letting Go of Past Guilt & Shame

When we are guilty of having done something wrong, it is normal and appropriate to have a sense of shame. That said, there are people who do horrible things, stupid things, behave disgracefully, behave rudely, and behave disrespectfully without feeling any shame. Not feeling shame at these times is often an indicator that the shameful behavior will continue.

When I was a teenager, I sometimes teased my younger sister about a physical characteristic she had no control over whatsoever: she was very skinny. I knew on some level that my teasing was mean and thoughtless, but it was not until later that I realized the negative impact it had on her self-image. I felt bad about it but carried the guilt and shame of what I did for many years without doing anything about it. Finally, many years into adulthood, I told her how sorry I was for what I had done and asked her for forgiveness. It had a healing effect on both of us.

The point is this: carrying shame and guilt without addressing it does not do you or anyone else any good. These feelings are only useful if we use them as a catalyst to change for the better. We do this by first going to our Creator and confessing without reservation how wrong we were. After asking Him for forgiveness, we must then sincerely apologize to those we have wronged with our behavior or attitudes, ask them for forgiveness, and do everything we can to redeem ourselves. Then we forgive ourselves.

After apologizing, restoring and redeeming ourselves, we need to move on, even if the wronged person cannot forgive us. At this point, it is of no service to anybody if we keep beating ourselves up and carrying guilt and shame.

We need to continue to do what is right and good, but we also must let go of the past guilt and shame that binds us.

Sometimes we feel that it is too late to ask for forgiveness or to restore. Perhaps we lost contact with the person we wronged because they've moved away, changed their number or are no longer on social media. They may have even passed away.

When I got married, my wife and I moved to the US, where we raised our family. I would call my parents every Sunday, and I continued to call my mother after my father passed away six years later. When my mother reached her mid-eighties, her health deteriorated; she suffered from dementia and it became more and more difficult to talk to her on the phone. Finally, it got to the point where she had to move to a nursing home and calls were impossible. For the next two years I wrote to her regularly and flew to Germany twice, but I felt sad that I could not visit her more often. Many times, as I sat at a campfire behind our house and played the harmonica to relax, I thought about my mother. With tears in my eyes I thought how nice it would be for her if she could be there sitting with me. In late December 2017 one of my sisters sent me an e-mail telling me that when she visited the nursing home, she found Mother crying. "I am waiting and waiting for my boy to visit me," she sobbed, "and he is not coming." That tore at my heart, and I thought about getting on a plane right then and there. However my other sister, who was more intimately involved with my mother and had a better understanding of dementia, told me that it would not make sense for me to travel to Germany for three days (which is all the time I had). She said our mother would not remember my visit the next day. What she said made sense, so I booked a flight for that summer when I would have more time. Then in February my mother fell and broke a hip. The stress of the pain, the required surgery and the physical therapy afterwards were too much for her. She passed away a couple of weeks later, leaving me not only mourning her death but feeling terrible that I had not visited her one last time.

I tell you this to show that we have a choice with regard to how we handle things we feel guilty about. My mother was gone, so my guilt would not serve her at all. Also, I had not intentionally done anything wrong, so I didn't need guilt or shame to "course correct." I knew she would forgive me, and I needed to forgive myself. Instead of wasting energy by beating myself up over it, I could redeem myself by visiting or calling an elderly person who was lonely or in a nursing home. I could let go of guilt and shame and use my energy to serve somebody else in a way that would please my mother.

In his prayer of repentance, recorded for us in the Psalms, King David gave us an example on how to move forward even after we have committed a grievous wrong:

"Wash me thoroughly from my iniquity, And cleanse me from my sin" (Psalm 51:2; NKJV).

As David did, we need to confess completely, without making excuses or minimizing the severity of what we have done, who we were, or what we have neglected. Then we ask for total forgiveness. If we show total remorse and don't hold back from taking full responsibility, God will not hold back His forgiveness. And then we should accept that forgiveness with our whole hearts.

Beating ourselves up over something that we can no longer change is not serving anybody. Now our focus must be on redemption, of building trust and patiently waiting for that trust to be restored, giving people time to accept that we have changed.

It is important to note here that many of us feel shame for things that were not our fault, such as those who have been abused. If this is the case with you, you must learn to let go of any of the shame you are holding. Seek any professional help you may need in order to do this, and know that if you lean on the Creator, He will help you to heal. "He heals the brokenhearted and binds up their wounds" (Psalm 147:3 NKJV).

To recap, when you have wronged someone and want to turn things around, focus on taking positive action now and in the future, rather than dwelling on the past. Let go of that guilt and shame that binds you, for it is unproductive and will not help anyone. Ask for forgiveness and trust that healing and freedom are possible when we let go and give it to God.

Questions to ask yourself:

- What guilt, shame or regret do I harbor in my mind?

  ____
  ____
  ____
  ____
  ____
  ____
  ____

- Is that shame based on something I have done, or something that was done to me (i.e. abuse)?

  ____
  ____
  ____
  ____
  ____
  ____
  ____

- How has past guilt or shame held me back and consumed much of my precious time and attention?

  ____
  ____
  ____
  ____
  ____
  ____
  ____

- What can I do to redeem myself?

____
____
____
____
____

- What can I focus on now to move forward?

____
____
____
____
____

- Can I accept that I cannot change the past?

____
____
____
____
____

- Will I do the best I can going forward?

____
____
____
____
____

- How can I use the pain as a catalyst for positive change?

____
____
____
____
____

CHAPTER 6

Letting Go of a Negative Self-Image

As mentioned earlier, people often assign the negative meanings cited in dictionaries to the word humility, rather than those faith-affirming definitions used in the Bible. This can carry over into the way they raise their children, which can lead to a lack of self-confidence in those children. While growing up, my five siblings and I did not receive a lot of praise from our parents, which was probably due to their own childhood experiences. My mother did not have a lot of self-esteem; and my father had a very strict mother who not only withheld praise but was so strict about his piano lessons that after her death when he was fourteen he never touched a piano again. Their unofficial motto when it came to childrearing was that "no complaint is enough praise"; their rationale was that not praising children much would keep them humble.

In the fifth grade I struggled to pass my English class, which was my first foreign language and required at my school. My

English teacher was an old lady who had also taught my mother decades earlier. Since my mother had never done well in her English classes, the expectation from the teacher was that I would not do well either. She offered me little to no encouragement, and that, coupled with my mother's struggle and my father's comment that he too was not competent in foreign languages, made me think that I was doomed to failure. I had a negative self-image with regard to learning a new language. Thankfully, as I grew older, I realized English would help me in any career and was thus motivated to learn it fluently. Though I did initially struggle, my grades started to improve when I let go of my low expectations and began to put forth more effort.

Once I decided to let go of the belief that I was not good at learning a foreign language, I mastered it! I realized it didn't have to be a struggle – all I had to do was read English language magazines and books, regularly listen to the news on American Forces Network, and travel to England during the summer. By the time I finished high school I had become one of the best students in my English class. Never in my wildest dreams, though, would I have imagined I'd one day write a book in English – yet here I am!

If we do not believe that we can become good at something and are doubting our God-given potential, we will not act! Without effort or action, we will not get results, or at least not the ones we want. Our poor results reinforce our lack of confidence, which further reinforces the lack of motivation to put forth any effort, because "what's the use anyway?" And the cycle continues.

Parents, teachers, coaches and other educators often do not praise children enough, not because of a lack of love, but because they never had good role models or received enough praise themselves. Another reason, as illustrated above, is that some have the mistaken belief that praising children will make them proud and arrogant. However, it has been my personal experience that praise helps to build confidence as well as a teachable and humble attitude.

Unlike humility and pride, humility and confidence are not mutually exclusive. As I write this chapter, I am on my way back from a seminar with the world's leading high- performance coach, Brendon Burchard. Meeting Brendon and the many attendants of his seminar confirmed to me that people with extremely high levels of competence and confidence can also be very humble. In fact, they continue to increase their level of confidence and competence because of their humility; they don't think they have "arrived" and therefore they continue to learn and to be taught and coached. So, you see, you can get rid of your negative self-image and lack of confidence and still have a deep sense of humility.

Consider the people around you. Those who have both confidence and humility are authentic; they are not easily offended and are usually a pleasure to be around. We can become that kind of person, if we let go of all the false beliefs that keep us hanging on to a negative self-image, beliefs which rob us of the confidence we need to fulfill our greatest God-given potential.

The biblical story of Jabez provides an excellent example of somebody who had a bad head-start in life and turned things around with prayer and a hopeful attitude.

"Now Jabez was more honorable than his brothers, and his mother called his name Jabez, saying, "Because I bore [him] in pain." (Talk about a bad head-start as far as self-image is concerned!) And Jabez called on the God of Israel saying, "Oh, that You would bless me indeed, and enlarge my territory, that Your hand would be with me, and that You would keep [me] from evil, that I may not cause pain!" So, God granted him what he requested" (1 Chronicles 4:9-10; NKJV).

Letting go of our negative self-image is one of the most liberating feelings we can experience. It helps us to unleash our full potential to live the life we are meant to live.

At another seminar, I heard Ethan Willis, author and CEO of Prosper, Inc., make this statement: "God does not call the qualified, but He qualifies the called."

Allow the truth of these words to settle into your heart. With God's help and strength, we will be able to become who He wants us to become and to accomplish what He calls us to do.

Questions to ask yourself:

- What negative images about myself have I been carrying with me?

  ____
  ____
  ____
  ____
  ____
  ____
  ____
  ____

- Has negative self-talk such as, "I can't do that"; "I don't have what it takes"; "That's not my personality"; or "I am too skinny, fat…et cetera" kept me back from the things I wanted to accomplish?

____

____

____

____

____

____

- What steps can I take to overcome the obstacles I have built in my own mind?

____

____

____

____

____

____

- What are the ten best character traits I possess?

____

____

____

____

____

____

- Where do those traits show up in my life?

____

____

____

____

____

- Can I exercise those traits in areas where I have not previously done so?

____

____

____

____

____

____

____

____

- What are the areas in my life in which I feel I've done well, and what made me do well in those areas? Can I transfer those success markers to more situations in my life?

____

____

____

____

____

____

____

____

- Am I giving myself and others the love (sometimes tough love) and encouragement I/we need to move in the right direction?

____

____

____

____

____

____

____

CHAPTER 7

Letting Go of the Past

We are who we are today based on what has happened in the past, be it of our own doing or the doing of others. Therefore, in order to become someone new, the someone we were meant to be, we must learn to let go of the past.

This is a tough one, especially when there is a lot of pain involved, as in the case of abuse or the loss of a loved one. Letting go of the past is even more difficult when we feel alone or that nobody understands us.

However, when we realize that our situation is not as unique as we think it is, and that others have gone through tremendous trials and losses and overcame them, we can find the inner strength to do the same.

I learned this while in Arizona, training to be certified as a High-Performance Coach by the High Performance Institute. Several of the other coaches shared their stories, and I listened in amazement to the unimaginable hardships they endured, and in awe of their positive energy and determination to move forward in their lives. It was truly humbling for me to see.

The Apostle Paul went through tremendous trials, as noted in his second letter to the church in Corinth:

> Are they ministers of Christ? – I speak as a fool – I [am] more: in labors more abundant, in stripes above measure, in prisons more frequently, in deaths often. From the Jews five times I received forty [stripes] minus one. Three times I was beaten with rods; once I was stoned; three times I was shipwrecked; a night and a day I have been in the deep; [in] journeys often, [in] perils of waters, [in] perils of robbers, [in] perils of [my own] countrymen, [in] perils of the Gentiles, [in] perils in the city, [in] perils in the wilderness, [in] perils in the sea, [in] perils among false brethren; in weariness and toil, in sleeplessness often, in hunger and thirst, in fastings often, in cold and nakedness – besides the other things, what comes upon me daily: my deep concern for all the churches (2 Corinthians 11:23-28; NKJV).

Paul also recounted his own responses to the above experiences in his letter to the Philippians:

> Be anxious for nothing, but in everything by prayer and supplication, with thanksgiving, let your requests be made known to God; and the peace of God, which surpasses all understanding, will guard your hearts and minds through Christ Jesus.

> Finally, brethren, whatever things are true, whatever things [are] noble, whatever things [are] just, whatever things [are] pure, whatever things [are] lovely, whatever things [are] of good report, if [there is] any virtue and if [there is] anything praiseworthy – meditate on these things (Philippians 4:6-8; NKJV).

I know of a man who within a few years lost his only daughter in a car accident then his wife to cancer. Talk about a lot of pain, not only for him, but for his daughter's son, who he was now raising alone. After losing two mother figures at such a young age, the boy turned to his grandfather and asked, "Can I have another mommy?" Despite his heartbreak, the man knew that to properly take care of his grandson he had to let go of the past and focus on building a happy future. Within a year or so, he started dating a lady he had known for a long time and they got married.

As you let go of loss, know that not everyone will approve. Some people believe that if we have resilience and can get over a loss relatively quickly, we don't care or are not honoring the dead. Moving on is nothing to be ashamed of. Everybody deals with grief differently, and there is no right or wrong way. We neither need the approval of others for how we deal with our loss, nor is it our place to tell them how to deal with theirs.

Having said that, if we can accept the loss of a loved one as the end of a season in our lives and the beginning of a new chapter, we can use that pain as an opportunity to grow. I remember the shift that occurred when my father passed away. Though by then I had been supporting myself for many years, and now had my own wife and children, somewhere in the back of my mind there was always this sense that if I really got into trouble my dad would help me out. With him gone, I was forced to rely more on God, the father who would take care of me when I needed it. This lesson was put to the test a few years later when I lost my job.

There was another positive shift that occurred as a result of my father's death. At his funeral I was profoundly affected by the eulogies given by his friends and colleagues. They spoke of the impact my father had on people through his volunteer work, something I had not previously been fully aware of. I remember telling my sister that I felt I did not have enough life left to make as much of a difference as he had. This prompted me to ask God to show me ways in which I could make a difference, and before I knew doors of opportunity, one of which is writing this book, began to open.

A few weeks ago, my wife and I spent our wedding anniversary watching videos of our kids when they were younger – on the beach, in the pool, and in the yard. As we did, we were filled with mixed emotions. On the one hand we were filled with gratitude and felt blessed that we were able to raise our children in a safe, clean, peaceful and healthy environment. On the other hand, I could not help but miss those times and felt a bit nostalgic and even sad that those days were in the past.

This example illustrates both the healthy and unhealthy ways we hang on to good things in our past. When we think about them in healthy ways, we focus on being grateful for what we had and allow ourselves to be filled with joy.

When we hang on to them in unhealthy ways, however, we are filled with longing and sadness that those people, things or circumstances are no longer there. The point is, we have a choice on what we focus on.

Questions to ask yourself:

- How much time do I spend thinking about the past?

- What do I think about when I am reminded of positive things that happened in the past? Do they fill me with gratitude and joy, or do I mourn the fact that those days are gone?

- When I am reminded of the painful and negative experiences of the past, where does my mind go? Have I identified memories of the past that make me sad, bitter, resentful, regretful?

- What lessons could I learn from those painful experiences?

- How can I think about the past in ways that would not make me bitter?

____

____

____

____

- Can I start to accept that the past cannot be altered, no matter how much I dwell on it?

____

____

____

____

- How does dwelling on the past keep me from being fully in the present? What lessons from the past can I use to help me be the best I can be in the present?

____

____

____

____

- Can I let go of the notion that building new relationships after a loved one dies is dishonoring them? Can I embrace the idea that it means I am resilient and moving forward? One word of caution here: when a spouse dies and there are children involved, any new relationship should be approached with the needs and the feelings of the children foremost in our minds.

____

____

____

____

CHAPTER 8

Letting Go of Grudges & Bitterness

During my seminars, grudges and bitterness have consistently emerged as the most challenging issues for people to let go of. They are also the most damaging. Grudges and bitterness are like a disease that rots every aspect of our lives – our relationships, families, marriages, and our very spirit – from the inside out. The cure for this disease is not necessarily easy, but it is simple: we need to let it go.

We all get into situations where we feel mistreated, disrespected, judged, condemned and hurt. Sometimes it is outright abuse and evil behavior on the part of another person, be it strangers and criminals, or those we are supposed to trust such as parents, teachers, aunts and uncles, pastors, siblings, grandparents, and so on. Other times, the "villain" does not intend to inflict the wound, but it hurts just the same.

Pain and suffering are nothing new; people have been hurting each other since humans walked the earth. However, while we cannot always avoid it, we can heal from it.

A perfect example still relevant today are the biblical stories of Cain and Abel, and Joseph and his brothers. One sibling receives more favor from the parents, leaving the other(s) hurt and resentful. That resentfulness builds against the favored sibling, whose only "fault" was that their behavior was more pleasing to the parent, the teacher or whoever it was that showed them more favor. While the conflict doesn't usually rise to the level of murder, the anger often becomes so strong that they want to undermine or hurt their siblings. At the very least, it makes a close relationship difficult, if not impossible.

Then there are those incredibly tough situations when real injury (i.e. a mugging or some other crime) is inflicted on us or somebody we love. It is completely understandable that we get angry and even fantasize about revenge against the perpetrator.

And then there are situations where people become resentful towards God, for example, for natural disasters in which they lose their homes or worse. The insurance industry even blames Him, calling these events "acts of God." We ask, "What kind of God would allow (fill in the blank) to happen?!" It is at these times when our very faith has been shaken to the core.

So, how are we to deal with those situations that have made us angry, resentful and even bitter?

There are basically two ways in which people deal with adversity and injustice, and neither has anything to do with the severity of the "injury." There are people who hold a lifelong grudge for a perceived offense; then there are those who have suffered tremendously at the hands of others and have been able to forgive. It all comes down to a choice.

1. Dealing with adversity unsuccessfully:

   The reason for holding on to grudges and bitterness always lies in the past. It gives us a false sense of control, and the false impression that our anger is somehow punishing the one who hurt us. While this response is both natural and understandable, it is also an irrational one. Why? It is irrational because (for the most part) it does not hurt the perpetrator, but you, the victim! Holding onto grudges and bitterness eats you up, causing a host of physical and emotional symptoms; in some cases, it even leads to death.

   As Nelson Mandela famously said, "Not forgiving is like drinking poison and expecting the other person to die."

   We also must remember that no matter what we do, we can never ever change what has happened in the past. Hanging onto it doesn't give us control; in fact, it ends up controlling us, and only keeps us stuck.

2. Dealing with adversity successfully.

   As with any challenging situation, the solution is one that helps us think clearly and rationally. I am not claiming that this is easy. But as the many people who have overcome unspeakable trauma will attest, it is possible.

   The key to letting go of grudges and bitterness is to learn how to forgive. But how does one learn this? And what does it mean to forgive anyway?

> If you look up forgive in English language dictionaries, you will see things like "to pardon"; "to grant relief"; "to stop feeling resentment against someone." As is the case with earlier examples in this book, I find these definitions to be both overbroad and a bit vague. Instead, what has helped me to deal with this subject is to have a look at what the Bible has to say about the topic of forgiveness.

Upon doing some research, I found that Hebrew, the language in which the Old Testament was originally written, has three different words that translate to the English "to forgive." The meaning of those words shed some light on what is required of us, for, as Jesus Christ said, "For if you forgive men their trespasses, your heavenly Father will also forgive you. But if you do not forgive men their trespasses, neither will your Father forgive your trespasses" (Matthew 6:14-15; NKJV).

The first Hebrew word for to forgive is *salah,* and it is used exclusively for God. Salah is translated into English as "forgive," "pardon," or "spare," but it is never applied to the kind of forgiveness a human can extend, only to something God does, for only God can forgive the guilt of our sins. When we hold on to a grudge and do not want to forgive a person, it does not have any effect on how God deals with that person.

God will serve justice and mercy independently of us. He can discern a person's heart much better than we can, so we can leave it up to Him to deal with an offender. "For we know Him who said, 'Vengeance is Mine, I will repay,' says the Lord. And again, 'The LORD will judge His people'" (Hebrews 10:30; NKJV).

The second Hebrew word translated as "to forgive" is *nasa.* This word literally means "to lift up"; "to carry"; or "to bear up." This verb is used for something both God *and* human beings can do.

Cain, who killed his brother Abel, said, "'My punishment is greater than I can bear (nasa).' It was a burden with which Cain did not feel he could cope. So God said to him, 'Therefore, whoever kills Cain, vengeance shall be taken on him sevenfold.' And the LORD set a mark on Cain, lest anyone finding him should kill him" (Genesis 4:13-15; NKJV).

In this case it was God who extended nasa to Cain; in other words, he lifted the tremendous burden from Cain's shoulders.

An example of a human being extending nasa was the story of Joseph.

> Thus you shall say to Joseph, 'I beg you, please forgive (nasa) the trespass of your brothers and their sin; for they did evil to you. Now, please, forgive the trespass of the servants of the God of your father.' And Joseph wept when they spoke to him (Genesis 50:17; NKJV).

This was a request for Joseph to lift a burden from his brothers, something they had carried around with them ever since they had sold Joseph into slavery. This burden also included the potential threat of retaliation for their actions. And Joseph graciously complied.

> Joseph said to them, 'Do not be afraid, for [am] I in the place of God? But as for you, you meant evil against

> me; [but] God meant it for good, in order to bring it about as [it is] this day, to save many people alive. Now therefore, do not be afraid; I will provide for you and your little ones.' And he comforted them and spoke kindly to them (Genesis 50:19-21; NKJV).

The third Hebrew word *is kaphar*. Its meaning is "to cover over," though it is also translated as to "reconcile"; "appease"; "pardon"; "purge"; and of course, "forgive." Like nasa, kaphar also describes an activity that both God and man can engage in. The way we can extend this kind of forgiveness is by not bringing up the wrongdoing of another person anymore. You learn from the past, but you move on from it.

Now, how do we deal with a situation in which somebody has done us so much harm that we consider them our enemies? Do we still forgive? Here is how we are supposed to deal with our enemies:

> You have heard that it was said, 'You shall love your neighbor and hate your enemy.' But I say to you, love your enemies… (Matthew 5:43-48; NKJV).

If right now you're thinking, *that is extremely hard,* you are not alone. Thankfully, the Bible provides further guidance. There are three things we are supposed to do:

1. "Bless those who curse you."

   "To bless" comes from the Greek word *eulogeo,* from which we get our English word eulogy. This means to say good things.

While they say bad things to us, we do not stoop down to their level, but say good things to them instead.

2. "Do good to those who hate you."

   This means we do not cause harm to others, even if they are our enemies. I know of siblings who fought so hard over an inheritance that they both lost, as one was bent on causing harm to the other. That's irrational behavior that hurts the self as much, if not more, than our enemy.

   Then there are the people who respond to hurtful acts with those of kindness, which oftentimes actually softens the heart of the perpetrator. I have experienced this myself. Somebody I had helped treated me very badly and said terrible things to me, yet with the help of God I was able to extend kindness towards that person, who then became very remorseful.

3. "And pray for those who spitefully use you and persecute you."

   We can go through the motions of saying good things and doing good things, but we can still carry a hateful attitude in our hearts. God wants us to pray, to make sure that our attitude is right before Him.

   And why are we supposed to do all this?

> That you may be sons of your Father in heaven; for He makes His sun rise on the evil and on the good, and sends rain on the just and on the unjust. For if you love those who love you, what reward have you? Do not even the tax collectors

> do the same? And if you greet your brethren only, what do you do more [than others]? Do not even the tax collectors do so? Therefore you shall be perfect, just as your Father in heaven is perfect (Matthew 5:45-48; NKJV).

God wants our attitude towards a wicked person to be like His:

> Say to them: "[As] I live," says the Lord GOD, 'I have no pleasure in the death of the wicked, but that the wicked turn from his way and live. Turn, turn from your evil ways! For why should you die, O house of Israel?' (Ezekiel 33:11; NKJV).

To summarize: Whether we forgive or don't forgive a person has nothing to do with their standing with God, or whether He forgives them or not. But it has everything to do with how it affects us in the here and now and also how our Creator will deal with us, when we come face to face with Him.

As I am writing this, it is the day of Passover, the day on which Jesus Christ went through tremendous pain and suffering to cover for my sins. Was that fair? Did He complain?

> For to this you were called, because Christ also suffered for us, leaving us an example, that you should follow His steps: "Who committed no sin, Nor was deceit found in His mouth"; who, when He was reviled, did not revile in return; when He suffered, He did not threaten, but committed [Himself] to

> Him who judges righteously; who Himself bore our sins in His own body on the tree, that we, having died to sins, might live for righteousness--by whose stripes you were healed (1Peter 2:21-24; NKJV).

To forgive does not mean we have to naively trust. Trust is earned or regained, which takes time and depends upon the other person's actions.

Once we have let go of our grudges and bitterness, we are free to move forward. A huge burden is lifted off our shoulders; we can have peace and also receive forgiveness from God.

Questions to ask yourself:

- Are there any grudges that I am holding on to?

  ____

- Do I understand what it means to forgive?

  ____

- Do I realize what holding on to grudges and bitterness does to me?

- Am I willing to let go of all grudges in my life?

- Have I any root of bitterness towards somebody or situation?

- Do I understand what it means to "love your enemy"?

- What excuses have I used to hold on to grudges?

- What excuses have I used for my bitterness?

- Do I have a victim mentality, or am I willing to take responsibility for my own life?

- When there is a problem, do I always see the other person as the villain?

- Can I be merciful to those who sin differently than I do?

- What inspiring books and stories can I read about people who have been able to forgive tremendous injustices and injuries?

- Will I allow those resources to put things into perspective for me and help me to see the benefits that come from letting go of grudges and bitterness?

CHAPTER 9

Letting Go of Being Stuck – Moving on to Serve Your Purpose

A year after Hurricane Katrina hit New Orleans, I heard an interview on the radio with a woman who was forced to get out of New Orleans because the house she lived in with her children had become uninhabitable. This was the case for many, but for this single mother it turned out to be a great blessing. She got away from the poverty-stricken and crime-infested neighborhood she had been unable to leave for various reasons. This tragic event turned out to be the catalyst she needed. Moving to a smaller, much quieter town in another state meant a new beginning and a much better future for her and her children. Letting go of the old enabled her to embrace something new.

Other people's circumstances are far more pleasant, but they are stuck, nonetheless. They live in a very nice place, but they live beyond their means, making themselves slaves to their property. As with the single mother from New Orleans, they could vastly improve their situation by letting go of this environment, for example, by downsizing or moving to a place with a lower cost of living. Of course, this is not always easy to do, for it feels like failure or giving up. They too may be on a collision course with a catastrophic event, in the form of mounting debts and mounting stress. Why wait for this to happen? Why waste time? When I was in that downward spiral, I had no time to waste, not even seconds. Had I held on to the controls of that plane any longer, I would have run right into the ground. Waiting to let go in many situations often makes things only harder and more difficult. Even if it takes us out of our "comfort zone," we need to consider letting go and moving on to a more suitable place. We can start taking steps to get us closer to where God wants us to be. We can cry out to Him in prayer and ask Him for His will in our lives.

That said, when considering a move, remember the old saying, "You take the weather with you." Sometimes, we may think we need to move away, and things will get better. It's important to make sure there is not something else that we need to let go of first.

Examining ourselves, our mindset, our motives, our attitudes, our level of forgiveness, our level of gratitude, our willingness to serve and to make sacrifices, and our ability to embrace a struggle – all those may reveal that the location we live in is not the problem, but the way we think.

Questions to ask yourself:

- Why do I want to get away from it all? When you have the answer to that question, ask "Why?" again, then ask "Why?" to that answer and so on. Ask this as many times as it takes until you find the motives of your heart at the deepest level.

  ____
  ____
  ____
  ____
  ____
  ____
  ____

- Do I live in a house, in a neighborhood, a town or an area of the country that I feel is bad for me and/or my family?

  ____
  ____
  ____
  ____
  ____
  ____
  ____

- Does my environment have negative pulls or temptations?

  ____
  ____
  ____
  ____
  ____
  ____

- Is where I live dangerous, harmful to my children, or harmful to my health?

____
____
____
____
____
____
____
____
____
____

- If any of this applies to me, how can I educate myself on my options (i.e. moving away)? For example, I can start doing some research to find out where I could go. I can also recognize that I may not be able to do this on my own and seek out help, for example from a non-profit organization or a social worker. Most importantly, I need to recognize if my uncomfortable situation has become my comfort zone and take action to get out of it.

____
____
____
____
____
____
____
____
____
____

- Am I living in an area that is beyond my means? If so, is this serving the needs of my family, or am I just keeping up with the Joneses?

- Do I serve my purpose where I am?

- Is there a plan, purpose, or desire to be where I am, or did I just happen to land here?

____
____
____
____
____
____
____
____

- If I don't love where I live, and though it may not have been my choice to be there, can I acknowledge that it may be where I am meant to be?
    - ❍ Does the place help me to grow and fulfill my purpose as a person?
    - ❍ Can I make a meaningful contribution to the community?

I believe that if those two criteria are fulfilled, we are in a good position to live a fulfilled life. Dietrich Bonhoeffer, who suffered greatly and eventually died for his resistance to the Nazi regime, wrote, "We can have a fulfilled life without all our dreams being fulfilled."

____
____
____
____
____
____
____
____

CHAPTER 10

Letting Go of a Job or Business

Are you happy with your career, whether you work for someone else or own your own business? If so, that is great, and I want to congratulate you because you are in a much better position than most people today.

Many years ago, I learned that like anything else, a job may not be all it's cracked up to be, and that in some cases, we have to let it go. As an engineering student in Germany, I had two semesters of internships, the first of which was right at the beginning of the program. I had the wonderful opportunity to live in Paarl in the Western Cape Province of South Africa, building machines for the wine industry. I was the first student from my engineering school who went overseas for this internship, and I was very excited.

Initially, the job was interesting, and I learned many new things, but soon it became boring. I was doing the same things over and over and began to feel that I was just used as cheap labor. In addition, the work environment was not friendly, and people were pressured to work a lot of overtime. The machines we were building had to be completed before the wine harvest, and it was crunch time. Of the fifteen people working there, more than half quit during the first ten weeks I was there.

Though I was not happy with the internship, I thought I had to stick with it. I needed to complete six months of practical machine shop experience as a prerequisite to start the engineering course work, and where else could I do this before the next semester started? Even if I found a place, it had to be approved by the college administration. Those were the days before the internet, so I couldn't just Google things or communicate via email, and overseas phone calls were too expensive, about one dime for every two seconds! Also, I felt that I had some obligation towards my mother's uncle, who had connected me with the owner of the company. I did not want my actions to reflect poorly on him. As you can see, there were many obstacles in my mind that prevented me from leaving the place.

Then tragedy struck and my uncle, a farmer in the neighboring country of Namibia, South West Africa, was killed in a helicopter crash. Ironically, he was the son of my mother's uncle, who had recommended me for the job. His death shook me to the core and made me reassess my situation. I had what some call "mortality motivation." I realized that life was too short to waste on an internship that I didn't enjoy and that didn't pay much. I started to think about what I could do to move forward and who I could talk to.

The woman who cut my hair happened to be married to a draftsman who used to work for the company. When I told her about the situation, she immediately understood why I wanted to leave; her husband had quit just a few weeks earlier. She invited me to talk to her husband. When I told him about my situation, he hooked me up with another machine building company he had worked for in the past. They called me in for an interview right away and offered me another job as an engineering intern. The next week, and the week after my uncle died, I quit my job with the first company. The new company was very nice to work for, gave me a lot of good experiences and even a bonus before I left.

It took a tragedy to shake me up, to make me take a step back, look at my situation and say, "This needs to change." That does not have to be the case with you.

It is easy to feel like we have no options, especially when we have obligations to meet, mouths to feed, and mortgages to pay. We also tell ourselves stories – often untrue – about the consequences of following our heart. Contrary to what I had feared, my mother's uncle completely understood why I left the company and did not hold it against me at all. Losing one of his sons had put things into a different perspective for him as well.

Sometimes we are just in a rut; our uncomfortable situation has become our comfort zone. Doing some brainstorming and research, and finding out what all our options are, is a necessary step in helping us get out of that rut. Letting go of a job or selling or closing a business can free us up to be at a place where we can contribute and feel good about it.

In the short term, making a move or making a change can be daunting, overwhelming, and thus more uncomfortable than staying where we are. To be happy in the long run, we need to summon our courage and take a step back, look at the big picture, and make choices to pursue what is important, meaningful and fulfilling to us.

Questions to ask yourself:

- Do I want to avoid the short-term discomfort of making a change and end up with the long-term pain of regret of staying stagnant? Or do I want to summon the courage to leave my comfort zone for long-term fulfillment and meaning in life?

  ____
  ____
  ____
  ____
  ____
  ____

- Does the stress and the time required to maintain my status quo rob me of good relationships, good health and happiness?

  ____
  ____
  ____
  ____
  ____
  ____

- Is it time to evaluate my situation and consider leaving, even if the business or the job pays well? What am I sacrificing?

  ____
  ____
  ____
  ____
  ____
  ____

- Do I have the courage to ask myself the serious questions and be brutally honest with myself? Questions like, what is the purpose of my business?

  ____
  ____
  ____
  ____
  ____

- Do I feel like I am a slave to my business? Do I own the business or does the business own me?

  ____
  ____
  ____
  ____
  ____

- If you inherited a business, you need to ask, Do I enjoy it, or am I just keeping up a family tradition? Will I be placing a burden on my children by expecting them to continue?

  ____
  ____
  ____
  ____
  ____

- Does the business serve the purpose of my life? Do I have a passion for it or feel like it serves my calling?

  ____
  ____
  ____
  ____
  ____

- What is the contribution to my family and/or community?

- Does the business leave me time for other things in my life that are important to me?

- Is my business an excuse to indulge my tendency to be a workaholic? Am I pouring myself into my business in an attempt to escape something or at the expense of other things I need to pay attention to?

CHAPTER 11

Letting Go of Personal Relationships

There is nothing more important in our lives than our relationships. Proactively seeking relationships that add purpose and meaning and allow us to contribute and to grow makes all the difference in our lives. Doing so, however, requires work and intention.

And, as is the case with habits, it also requires us to let go of those relationships that are non-productive or destructive.

Many years ago, an elder of my church asked me to reach out to a man who had left a message on the church's answering machine. The man had a German accent, and since I was born and raised in Germany, the elder thought we would communicate more easily. I called him up and indeed, we had a very interesting conversation. The man, who was about thirty years my senior, had a fascinating background and seemed to share many of my values and beliefs. I wound up inviting him and his wife to our church and we had them over to our house for dinner several times.

At first glance, the man appeared to have a lot of interesting thoughts, ideas and wisdom. But over time I began to see that he had major issues. He was very critical of everybody who was successful in life (he had not accomplished much); he was also a know-it-all and rather abusive to his wife and family. He had five adult children, one of whom had tragically committed suicide and the other four wanted nothing to do with him.

I challenged him with some questions to which he was not receptive and became disagreeable. In the end, the relationship did not seem to serve either one of us.

For the sake of his poor wife, my wife stayed in touch with her until she passed away. He tried to put a guilt trip on me for cutting off my relationship with him, but I felt I needed to put my energy into relationships that were positive and beneficial.

This was not the case with his wife who, despite his abuse, never had the courage to leave him and live with her children as they had suggested. He used religion and her upbringing, in which divorce was never an option, to shame her into staying with him. It wasn't until her death that she was finally free of him.

In setting boundaries in our relationship with others, we may come to a point where letting go is the best option. That takes courage, but it's worth considering, as it can liberate us for positive development and growth producing relationships.

The following examples from the Bible clearly illustrate when we should consider letting go of relationships. As is stated in

Proverbs 12:26, NKJV: "The righteous should choose his friends carefully, For the way of the wicked leads them astray."

- Abusive relationships.

  We must never tolerate abuse. We need to seek relationships that build us up and help us grow rather than those which pull us down.

- Relationships that distract us from our purpose.

  Each of us is called to fulfill a purpose. Not fulfilling that purpose for which we are designed is a waste of the time God gave us, and if other people are holding us back from fulfilling it we need to let them go or limit their influence and presence in our lives.

- Relationships that take us away from our relationship with God.

  Our relationship with our Creator is the most important relationship we can have. A big part of who I am is a result of my relationship with Him. This is a relationship for all eternity. I depend on Him completely with everything. If somebody cannot respect that and tries to discourage me from faithfully following our Heavenly Father to the best of my understanding, their role in my life will be greatly reduced. We must never give in to people who pressure us to violate our conscience. I found myself in such a situation in, of all places, a church. I imagined the time when I would face my Creator; I imagined Him asking me why I had acted against my conscience. The only answer I would have was, “I followed them,” to which He would reply, “Why did you not follow Me?” At that moment it became crystal clear that I had to distance myself from people who tried to control and manipulate me in a way that would have put a wedge between God and me.

We may also need to let go of relationships with people who ridicule and make fun of what is right and what is precious to our Heavenly Father and to us. We do not need to hang around people who show that kind of disrespect, not because of our ego, but to protect our precious relationship with God.

- Dating relationships that do not share our highest values

  I remember a long solo drive I took through the Namib Desert, in Namibia, South West Africa back in 1980. I was twenty-one years old and driving my ten-year-old Volkswagen Beetle; there was no radio reception and I encountered only three other cars the entire day. I was all alone in God’s creation, with plenty of time to think, plenty of time to reflect. It felt great. When I reached Windhoek, I checked into a hotel and headed to the bar to have a beer. There were other people there, and though I talked with them I felt lonely. I did not have much in common with them. I learned then that I would much rather be alone than with people who had no respect for my values, including my faith.

  Aunt Ursula was somewhat of a role model in this regard. She was engaged once, broke it off and remained single for the rest of her life. Such was the case for many women of her generation, as so many men were killed in action during World War II. But Ursula was never alone. When she passed away, so many people came to the funeral, that the police had to direct traffic, which is something I had never seen in Germany before unless it involved a celebrity. She was always visited by people, including young people when she was in a nursing home. Throughout her life, she spent time and maintained good relationships with nephews, nieces, friends and other family members. She continuously grew her circle of friends. Aunt Ursula reminded me that it was better to be single than to settle, and it was a lesson I carried into my late thirties when I married my wife. We have been happy together for twenty-three years.

My aunt's story reminds me of that quote, mentioned earlier, by Friedrich Bonhoefer, a minister who died in a concentration camp: "You can have a fulfilled life without all your dreams being fulfilled."

When it comes to marriage, this has been my motto: Better to have a dream that is never fulfilled than a nightmare that becomes reality!

- Letting go of negative peer pressure.

  It is human nature to adjust our standards according to the expectations of our closest peers. Our peers either lift us up or tear us down. We need to recognize if the influence of peers is negative and stop it. Beware of groupthink; for example, the saying "Take one for the team" is often used as an excuse for compromising one's own convictions. It is often used to squelch independent-minded and critical thinkers among us.

Questions to ask yourself:

- Are there relationships in my life that are abusive? It is time to get out of those immediately.

- Do I have relationships with people who are always complaining, always negative and are just a drain on my time, my mental, emotional and spiritual energy? What keeps me in those relationships?

- Do I have relationships which neither serve me nor the other person, but take away time that I could be spending with people who help me grow?

- Have I been dating somebody for a long time without making a commitment? Is there something that holds me back or holds them back from doing so? It may be time to make a tough decision.

- Am I more scared about being lonely than about being tied to the wrong person? Can I think of ways to grow old as a single person without being lonely?

- Am I allowing people to pressure me into relationships I do not really want or care for?

- Are there relationships in my life in which no amount of goodwill and effort on my part makes them productive or meaningful?

- While I cannot choose my relatives, do I have the courage to decide how much time I spend with them?

CHAPTER 12

Letting Go of Associations / Organizations

Have you ever been part of an organization, such as a hobby club, a professional association, a networking group or a religious group? You usually sit in the same seat and you know the people next to you. You are not stressed because they are similar to you; they don't challenge you or expect much of you. You are in your comfort zone.

Then, at some point, you may start to notice that this feeling of comfort becomes more of a feeling of constraint. Perhaps you have moved on with your life and your focus or perspective is different from that of the association, or perhaps every meeting is the "same old, same old," and you have just grown tired of it. Whatever the case, you are no longer satisfied.

My family and I have moved a couple of times over the years due to my job situations, and part of that process was finding new church fellowships. It was a given that prospective fellowships would have a set of core beliefs with which we agreed;

in addition to this however, I also kept in mind the advice of a wise friend: "When you look for a fellowship, look for a place where you can grow and where you can make a contribution." More than once, we would join fellowships that seemed to meet these criteria, only to find over time that people became very controlling and insistent on doing everything their way.

I do not like to manipulate or control people, nor do I want to be controlled and manipulated. I do not allow it, especially when it comes to acting against my best understanding and my conscience. There I will not compromise, and neither should anybody else. God expects us to walk uprightly with integrity of heart for His ways.

When we find ourselves in these situations – either because we feel oppressed or merely stagnant – we have a choice to make: stay comfortably stuck, or say goodbye and move on. If we choose the latter, we must let go completely, including any hurt feelings, grudges, and bitterness about any wrongs, perceived or actual, that were done to us. It is only when we adopt an attitude of grace and forgiveness that we will truly be free and open to associations in which we can grow and make a greater contribution according to God's purpose for our lives.

When we are deciding to leave an association, a key consideration is the impact the other members have on our mindset. Our minds often mirror our surroundings, and the standards we have in our minds subconsciously adjust to those of the people we spend time with. If we want to be healthy, we need to surround ourselves with health-conscious people. If we want to be a high achiever, we need to surround ourselves with high achievers. If we want to quit smoking or quit any other habits, we need to spend more time with people who either do not have those habits or have overcome them.

Questions to ask yourself:

- Am I growing in this association or organization? Does it contribute to either my personal growth or skill development?

- Am I of real service here? Am I making a significant difference?

- Does this association serve what I believe to be my calling? Or does it take time and other resources away from what I am really meant to do?

- Does my association make it harder for me to break habits I want to break?

- Do I need to free up some time to spend with people who are striving for a life that is more closely aligned with my values and what I want to accomplish and contribute?

CHAPTER 13

Letting Go of Certain Traditions

What differentiates the many diverse cultures of the world from each other? To a large degree, it is the traditions that each has developed over the decades, centuries or millennia. One definition of culture, which I heard in a seminar, has always stuck with me: "Culture is the sum of the things which we take for granted" – in other words, it is those traditions we observe without question. Traditions certainly have their place in every culture, for they are a source of continuity, stability, sense of identity and belonging.

Having traveled extensively and worked with people from all over the world, I've had the opportunity to know many different cultures and their traditions. This has made me look at various traditions I grew up with from a different perspective. And when my wife (who is from Canada) and I immigrated to the United States, we saw traditions that we liked and which made sense to us, and others that did not make much sense at all.

One of the American traditions I really like is Thanksgiving, for the simple fact that showing gratitude for our many blessings is one of my core values. In fact, to be grateful is a universally recognized value in most cultures around the globe. Gratitude goes hand in hand with humility and serves us well in our relationship with our Creator as well as our fellow man.

Halloween, on the other hand, is a tradition I do not care for at all. I can see why some people like it, for it is associated with some fun childhood memories, however, as someone from a culture where it was never practiced I simply cannot find any humor in spooky costumes or haunted hayrides. It seems to me to be promoting ugliness and making fun of death, not to mention plying children with a whole lot of sweets that are not exactly part of a healthy diet.

The point is, while there are traditions that hold great value, the fact that something is a tradition does not necessarily mean it has value. As with everything in life, it is prudent for us to evaluate for ourselves. For example, does the tradition promote values such as brotherly love, respect, honor, humility, gratitude, and service? If so, then it certainly makes sense to keep it!

However, if a tradition has become a burden to you and others, you should consider letting go of it. Some traditions that come to mind as particularly stressful include the shopping frenzy that takes place during Christmastime, very elaborate wedding feasts, or others that require an output of resources we cannot afford. Let go of traditions that do not promote positive values like love and respect and instead promote a prideful "us versus them" mindset.

This may be difficult at first, or at best uncomfortable. After all, traditions are called such because a group participates in them unquestioningly, so you may see pushback when you try to leave the herd. If you can get past this, however, and stick to your decision, you will find it extremely liberating.

When deciding if you should let go of a tradition, it basically comes down to whether it resonates with who you are or want to be. Is your identity tied to some manmade construct, or is it based on the fact that you are a child of God, who strives to promote peace between people; serve other people; treat them with respect and love and to be forgiving rather than holding grudges; to be filled with humility instead of pride?

Religious institutions are not immune from this consideration, as some religious traditions have promoted violence and divisiveness. Should not such traditions promote values such as peace, forgiveness, mercy, patience, and so on?

When looking at religious traditions, I am thinking of what Jesus Christ said about them: "…Why do you also transgress the commandment of God because of your tradition?" (Matthew 15:3; NKJV)

Clearly, Jesus was not pleased with certain traditions that were kept during His time.

"And in vain they worship Me, Teaching [as] doctrines the commandments of men"; "For laying aside the commandment of God, you hold the tradition of men--the washing of pitchers and cups, and many other such things you do." He said to them, "[All too] well you reject the commandment of God, that you may keep your tradition." (Mark 7:7-9; NKJV).

Traditions are often followed just to fit in, even when people do not like them. We need to ask ourselves, is fitting in more important than doing what is right? Do not cave to peer pressure and uphold traditions that prevent you from being free to fulfill your highest potential and make your greatest contribution while on this earth.

Our sense of stability, security and continuity should come from our close relationship with God, not from holding on to traditions.

Traditions have their place and can provide some structure. But they must have a purpose and they must be subordinated to our highest values.

Questions to ask yourself:

- Are there things that I do simply for tradition's sake?

- Do I feel obligated to follow certain traditions, even though they make no sense to me?

- Are there traditions that may have served society well in the past, but due to changes in technology have become obsolete?

- Are there religious traditions I hold onto that have more to do with culture than spiritual values?

____

____

____

____

____

____

____

____

____

____

____

____

____

____

- Do I put up with traditional practices that are harmful and senseless, such as certain initiation rites?

____

____

____

____

____

____

____

____

____

____

____

____

____

CHAPTER 14

Letting Go of Stereotypes

There is a tendency in our society to give everybody a label and categorize them as part of a specific group. This is how we identify people, so when we encounter people from a specific group, the sum of the encounters with people from that group forms our opinions about that group. This then becomes our expectation when we meet new members of that group. We form a stereotype.

In 1980, when I took that internship in Paarl, South Africa, apartheid was still the law of the land. Like everyone else I had read much about it, and so I arrived in that country with a lot of pre-conceived ideas about its problems and how they could be solved. If everybody would just ignore skin color, I thought, things would work out just fine. I came to realize, however, that the situation was a lot more complex and complicated than I ever imagined. South Africa is a microcosm of the world, a country where people from all over have migrated to over the centuries, resulting in tremendous ethnic and cultural diversity.

While there, I had the opportunity to live and work with people of different ethnic and cultural backgrounds, and I observed that certain traits and cultural norms were more dominant in some ethnic groups than in others. My exposure to the various groups helped me to overcome some prejudices about people, as those prejudices were not consistent with what I saw in the people I got to know. However, I must admit that at the same time, I also developed stereotypes for ethnic groups that I had never been much exposed to before.

Thankfully, when I came to the US as an exchange student a couple of years later, I became close friends with people from the same ethic group about which I had developed a negative stereotype. Their personality and character traits were just the opposite of what I had experienced before. This taught me to never assume that all people are a certain way just because of their ethnic or cultural background.

Stereotypes can go both ways. A few years ago, I encountered a family from Germany who we wanted to help settle in America. Based on what I was told about the family but also to a large degree based on their background, I had very high expectations with respect to work ethic, cleanliness, an eye for quality, and so on. Boy, was I disappointed! They did not live up to any of the stereotypes, albeit positive ones, I had held in my mind.

It is natural to trust people more if they have backgrounds similar to ours. We believe we know what to expect of them, because they appear to be within our comfort zone. This, however, is not rational.

What I learned is that I need to let go of my stereotypes and consider each person as an individual rather than a member of a group. This leaves me open to get to know him or her based on their words and actions, rather than on my own assumptions. I learned that when we pigeonhole people, we are limiting both them and ourselves; we are closing ourselves off to potentially great relationships.

Even though there are cultural differences between people and certain characteristics may be more dominant in some cultures than in others, each person is different, and some do not fit the mold we try to put them in at all.

Letting go of stereotypes helps us to see people more clearly, and from a higher perspective. It opens our minds to develop relationships with people where before there existed only barriers. Groupthink, on the other hand, creates an "us versus them" mentality and robs us of our objectivity with regard to others. In order to connect with that objectively, we must simply recall Martin Luther King Jr.'s "I Have a Dream" speech, when he spoke of a future when we would all judge a person based on the content of their character rather than their appearance.

Personally, the best part of letting go of stereotypes has been finding the love of my life from across the globe. Despite our different national origins, we had an instant meeting of the minds to a degree I had never experienced before. Our two boys, who were born in the US, have triple citizenship – American, Canadian and German. Some people might think that is confusing, but when I asked our older son at the age of three, "Are you an American?" he said "No!" I then asked, "Are you

Canadian?" and again he said "No!" I then asked, "Are you German?" and yet again he said "No!" Finally, I asked, "Well, what are you then?" Emphatically and with confidence, he said, "I am David!"

I think my young son innately understood the sentiment the Apostle Paul expressed in his letter to the Philippians: "… our citizenship is in heaven…" (Philippians 3:20; NKJV).

Letting go of stereotypes may be easier if we understand that love has no boundaries, because the one who created us all *is* love! "He who does not love does not know God, for God is love" (1John 4:8; NKJV).

Questions to ask yourself:

- What stereotypes have I developed in my own mind?

- Do I tend to pigeonhole people based on their background or very superficial knowledge I have about them?

- Have I built walls in my mind that have kept good people away from me just because they were from a different group or background?

- Am I quick to blame a certain group for something that a member of that group may have done?

____
____
____
____
____
____
____
____

- Am I more tolerant of the shortcomings of a person who I consider "one of us" than a person who is "one of them"?

____
____
____
____
____
____
____
____

- Am I quick to judge people as "guilty by association"?

____
____
____
____
____
____
____
____

CHAPTER 15

Letting Go of Trappings

We all have a certain image of ourselves in mind. There is the person we think we are, then there is the person we would like to be and the person we want others to think we are.

Depending on how confident we feel, we express ourselves the way we are. We wear the clothes we like; we drive the car we like; we decorate our homes the way we like it, and so on. At least we like to think that's what we do. Or, do we care about the latest fads or what image we are portraying to others?

If we lack confidence, we may be led by other people's opinions on what is cool or what advertisements suggest we buy. Even if we think of ourselves as confident, we often still adopt a certain style based on an image we like to identify ourselves with. We may deceive ourselves that maintaining a certain style makes a difference in how we are truly living. I know, I have been there. Buying that SUV after getting married made me feel like that old boy scout in me had come back to life.

When we think about it, though, we realize that driving a Jeep does not make us a rugged outdoorsperson; and driving a Volvo Station Wagon does not make us a college professor. Having worked in the automotive industry most of my life, I always think of cars as an example.

I took driving lessons back when the first generation of the Volkswagen Golf came out, replacing the legendary VW Beetle as the "entry level vehicle" many Germans drove after World War II. The Golf Hatchback was considered a cool vehicle for young people, while older, retired people preferred the sedan version, the VW Jetta. You would rarely see a young person driving a Jetta, so when I came to the US as an exchange student, I was surprised to see that the Jetta was considered a cool car for college kids. How funny; it was all in the eyes of the beholder.

Personally, I always liked station wagons, even when I was single. Friends told me that those were not cool, that I couldn't impress the girls with them, and that I would remain single for the rest of my life. Why did I like a station wagon? It was practical. I had all the space I needed, even when I took a skiing trip with my friends or gave other people rides. I wanted to serve, and it was a perfect fit for me.

Turns out that when I met my future wife, she told me that she'd always wanted a guy with a station wagon, not a sportscar. Now *I* thought that was cool! Had I driven a sports car to portray an image of somebody I was not, I would not have attracted the right person, who wanted me for who I was. I would have attracted the wrong person, who was interested in the false image I was trying to project. I would have had to keep up maintaining that false image, which would have been stressful and likely a disaster!

What has made our relationship so special is that from the very beginning my wife and I felt completely at ease with each other. We could simply be who we are, with total authenticity and no pretense. It was the real deal…genuine.

If we are not liked and loved in a relationship for who we really are, we will never be happy. That said, we can oftentimes feel trapped by our ego or the false expectations of others and seek to fulfill those expectations by fitting into a particular mold. We can liberate ourselves by shifting our focus to who our best selves really want to be and what truly matters in life.

An excellent, albeit unfortunate, example of this is a fancy wedding I once attended. It had all the elaborate trappings – great food, great entertainment, a very well-dressed bridal party, and dancing well into the night. Clearly, they had spared no expense. When the couple divorced six months later, I couldn't help but wonder if all the focus had been placed on the wedding celebration, rather than on the marriage.

Even a nice family get-together at Thanksgiving can cause a lot of stress if the focus is on the trappings (i.e. the perfect turkey, baked, grilled or smoked, exactly as we think it should be; side dishes; the perfectly color-coordinated decorations, fancy china and silverware; matching napkins with a turkey printed on them, and of course the pie exactly like Grandma made it, nothing else will do). All the focus on preparing the trappings can take our minds away from thinking about how we can show up as our best selves, doing our best to connect with family and friends. Bringing joy, gratitude, and an uplifting positive energy to the gathering will be remembered and cherished not only in the moment, but long after we have forgotten how the food tasted and what the decorations looked like.

Remember that trappings entrap us! All that stuff is just props, not the real deal!

Questions to ask yourself:

- How much attention do I pay to the trappings in my life?

  ____
  ____
  ____
  ____
  ____
  ____
  ____
  ____

- Which of these trappings do I need to let go because they are simply not worth my time, energy, money, space or any other resource?

  ____
  ____
  ____
  ____
  ____
  ____
  ____
  ____

- What trappings do not reflect who I am? Do I have trappings which add to a false image?

- Do my trappings hide my true self?

- Do some of my trappings create pretense or a façade in my life?

- Do I focus more on image than relationships?

CHAPTER 16

Letting Go of Stuff

Do you sometimes wish you had less stuff accumulated in your house, in your life? You are probably not a hoarder, but you still find it hard to get rid of things you have not even used in years. The following will give you some food for thought on how to liberate yourself, as well as your children or heirs, from all your stuff. We all know that we cannot take stuff with us anyway. As I once heard somebody so eloquently quip, "I have never seen a U-Haul Trailer behind a hearse."

During my father's career as a contract lawyer, he helped a lot of people write their last will and testament. Many of them did not have somebody they trusted to become the executor of their will, so my father referred them to one of his trusted colleagues. In return, whenever they helped somebody with their testament, they would refer them to my father to become the executor of their wills. When he retired, people who had been referred to him over the years passed away and he would become the executor of their wills. Several situations arose where there were either no relatives to look after the estate, or they lived too far away. In such cases my father would go through their stuff, sort out what was valuable and forward it to the heirs. Other things, such as furniture and household goods that the relatives did not want, were given to charity. On a few occasions my dad hired me and some of my friends to rent a truck and haul things away to a charity warehouse or a junkyard.

Based on this experience, my parents decided that they would not want their children to go through the arduous process of sorting through their stuff when they passed away. Each year they would alternate between the attic and the basement, going through everything stored there. Anything they had not used for two years was either given away or thrown away. It was an amazing thing to behold.

It can be an emotionally draining experience to sort things out, especially if these things have sentimental value. At the same time, it can be very liberating, helping us to let go of the past and move forward in life. We can ask ourselves, does hanging on to the past prevent me from being fully present in the here and now? While the sorting process is often like taking a sentimental walk down memory lane, the result will be a clean, decluttered environment, in which we can focus on what we want in our lives. I know it's not easy; in fact, even as I am writing this, I realize that I still have books from college that I have not looked at in over thirty years! It's time to get rid of them and make room for what is important now.

When I went back home to Germany for my mother's funeral a couple of years ago, I spent a few days with my sister clearing out Mother's place. There was still a lot left, and it was an emotional time. The fact that she had already sorted out many things certainly made it a lot easier for my siblings and me.

There were some things that I would have loved to keep. Heirlooms, such as my father's old mechanical typewriter that he used until the end of his life, and my mother's traditional costume, which she wore at very special occasions including my wedding. But I knew those things would just be stuck somewhere in a cabinet or the attic and never ever be used again. My sister and I donated them to a local heritage museum, where they are still on display for others to enjoy.

If you are faced with the choice of getting rid of a lost loved one's mementos, ask yourself, "What would honor my mother/father/spouse, et cetera more – keeping a lot of his/her stuff around me and reminiscing about the past, or visiting an elderly or sick person who can hardly get out of the house or the nursing home? What would make the greater impact? What would be more meaningful in the here and now? And what would give me a greater sense of fulfillment?"

"...but lay up for yourselves treasures in heaven, where neither moth nor rust destroys and where thieves do not break in and steal" (Matthew 6:20; NKJV).

We can be slaves to things we have. We are so busy protecting and maintaining them that we have less time for what is more important – our relationships with God, family and friends. Ask yourself whether making the money to buy it, maintaining it, insuring it, cleaning it, and so on takes more time than what it is worth in terms of enjoyment, relationship-building or serving. As I write this, I can't help but think of all the boats and swimming pools that require a lot of upkeep and are hardly used.

Does the thing serve us and others; or does it just serve an image we are trying to maintain? When surveyed about what they like the most about their cars, many Ferrari owners replied, "The looks I get from other people."

I am a real estate investor, and in one of the courses I took one of the noted advantages of real estate investing was "pride of ownership." If pride of ownership is needed to give us a sense of significance, what does that say about our relationship with God? Again, our sense of significance should come from our awareness of the fact that we are children of the most powerful and most loving being in the entire universe and our service to Him. Let go of trying to impress others with your possessions and focus on pleasing your Creator. What others think of us should only be relevant with respect to us setting a good example and glorifying God in who we are and what we do.

Questions to ask yourself:

- What things have I not used at all in the last two years?
    - Are they of any value?
    - If so, who can use them and benefit from them more than I?

- What books have I read and will never read again?

- What books do I have and don't plan to read?

- What is the cost of keeping things in terms of time, money, energy and space versus the benefit those things still provide?

- Is pride of ownership my motive?

- Am I sure that my heirs would really want what I have kept for them? If so, why not give it to them now?

- How would getting rid of things simplify my life and free me up for what is important to me now?

- If I want to keep something to remind me of a person or a pleasant experience, would a picture of that thing serve the same purpose?

Conclusion

I hope that this book has inspired you to look within yourself, discover what has been holding you back and begin to let them go so you can move forward and grow. This is not instantaneous, of course, but a process that will require courage and patience. It will also require you to relinquish the controls you have been fighting to hold onto most of your life.

My hope and prayer for you is that you will feel truly liberated when you let go and allow God to do what you cannot do for yourself. Nothing feels more comforting than being carried in the loving arms of our Creator. That's the feeling I had sitting in the cockpit of the Cessna 150, when He carried me as on eagle's wings back safely to the ground.

Letting go clears our minds and our lives from clutter so we can continue to learn and grow and fulfill our purpose in life. When I lost a job and started a business relatively late in life, I remembered what the late Jim Rohn, a legend in personal development, said: "When you own a business, work harder on yourself than you work on your business." I have taken this to heart and embarked on a journey, not only to develop skills relevant to my business but also grow as a person in other areas. In addition to reading books about skill and personal development, I also hired a Certified High-Performance Coach to assist me. Going through this process has changed my life; in fact, I enjoyed it so much that I decided to train and become certified in high performance coaching myself.

I guide my coaching clients through the process of letting go of baggage, both the kinds I describe in this book and various other things humans tend to cling to out of a need for stability. Everything in this book is common sense, however, common sense is not always common practice, and that's where I come in. I provide my clients with the tools to become the best version of themselves and be fulfilled by serving and contributing at their highest level.

To learn more about our one-on-one coaching, group coaching, seminars, and keynote addresses, please visit our website www.carriedoneagleswings.com.

Soar on Eagles Wings,
Reinhard Klett, CHPC
reinhard@carriedoneagleswings.com